Some
Me
Time

. . . Making Caring for Yourself a Habit!

CHANDINI ANN KHANNA

PARTRIDGE

To order additional copies of this book, contact
Toll Free 800 101 2657 (Singapore)
Toll Free 1 800 81 7340 (Malaysia)
orders.singapore@partridgepublishing.com

www.partridgepublishing.com/singapore

I have what seems to be the most envied – time. Time to work, cook, help…..just no time for myself!

At some point all of us or most of us at all times, feel rushed and behind, what we have laboriously written up as a schedule. We make time for mundane tasks, routines; time for business and office associates, necessary time to eat, drink and sleep.

Stop to think though, how many minutes or seconds in the day, do we spend for 'me'. We are at a loss to answer that question.

Sure all we do is tremendously important, even life-saving at times but doesn't 'me' need time too.

Stop. Breathe. Relax. Focus on 'me'. Give 'me' a pat on the back and smile. An energized 'me' is a countless times more effective 'me'

God in his wisdom meant for us to like ourselves first, so who are we to question that!

It is but a fallacy that the world with its passive aggression and sullenness will attempt to make us feel any better. The sordid truth is that the goodness & simplicity that were once in abundance are being nibbled away by negative influences.

The very fact that we need to stop and consciously make 'me' time paints a sorry picture.

We all have our personal beliefs and ideals that we so vociferously guard. We try even harder to mirror them on the people we come in contact with.

Hilariously we even broadcast these beliefs on social networking sites. All in an effort for people to see the real 'me'. We feel elated and the ego gets a boost when those announcements are acknowledged. And I dare say we are livid when they are ignored. ☺

Funny creatures we are – we don't make 'me' time and yet are infuriated when people who don't matter ignore and don't place 'me' on a pedestal.

It will be a futile attempt and a shameful waste of space to delve on the various emotional, psychological and physiological disruptions that this ignoring of 'me' brings. We read those sordid tales often enough or hear them as examples of those around us.

This book is not about that or any magical cure. It is a humble attempt to veer your attention to the all-important 'me' .

How many of us will read this book, nod our heads in agreement and promise to make 'me' time. And then the obvious will happen – with the book out of your sight, 'me' gets pushed to where it shouldn't be – the back of your head, lowest on your list of priorities.

The humongous sea of people that one is surrounded by, never once have I heard of anyone having ever made a New Year Resolution that said – "I will make some 'me' time". Make that resolve now!

If the 'me' is neglected you can be sure that sooner than later, you will slip up or neglect a number of important details and soon find your world standing on its head.

I found my world upside down too and in my rush to pick up the bits that fell out, I ignored 'me'. Consciously and summoning all my faculties, I made 'me' time. Slowly at first and then at a quicker pace, life came back to standing on its feet and has inspired me to write about it.

This little book is meant to carry you through your days – some tedious, others happier – through clarity and brevity of thought.

The thought that you don't need to attend classes, seminars or pour over preachy books to get through and understand your life, should be the boost you need.

The root cause and its solution lie in just knowing, loving and taking time out for 'me'. It is easy, quick and free – anytime of the day!

You will notice a quantum leap – your confidence, happiness and quality of life in general. You owe it yourself – start with this and move on to experiencing every good thing life has to offer.

'Me' time is your right and responsibility – to re-invent yourself constantly, lest someone else takes control.

Have some bodacious fun in your 'me' time. Do what you wouldn't otherwise do or have the time to do. And you know in your deepest recesses what it is exactly that you want to do. How every fiber in your body is struggling for that to come to the fore.

It's possible – just focus on getting the 'me' time.

There are times in the day, almost every day, when I know that I probably don't deserve anything that I have received. It is overwhelming and humbling.

This thought has the ability to pull me down but my savior is always 'me' time. Clearing my head puts things in perspective and restores the balance of the internal and external.

At the risk of sounding cynical, I add that the world will not stop its unabashed exploitation of character, corrosion of feelings and its deafening silence to emotions. It becomes even more imperative for each one to dig deep, remain grounded and unperturbed.

This is only possible through an inner strength and confidence that is deep rooted and not available from the outside.

When was the last time you had the courage, yes courage, to lay on your back basking in the radiance of the winter sun or under the gaze of the stars on a cool cloudless night? You thinking of nothing - You, just you, without the myriad thoughts, countless gadgets and the unceasing sounds from around!

It's probably hard for you to recall since it's been so long or probably never happened. Some of you might even be shocked by the suggestion.

This should be your wake up call. The alarm bells should ring loud and clear to wake you up from this faux slumber.

Grab some 'me' time to appreciate the simple pleasures which are now so few and far between.

My thoughts would have probably remained my own, had I not listened to the little voice in my head that spoke in 'me' time.

All of us have that voice which tries to teach us, beckons us and nudges us to do what is good for us spiritually, emotionally and would also be great for the psyche.

We often don't listen, don't heed and just rush through everything that life lays out for us. ☹

Saying so is not to be interpreted as being lazy or sluggish. It is the boost we need to look internally and discover that all you need to be strong is WITHIN YOU. Just pause and listen. No one else can do this for you.

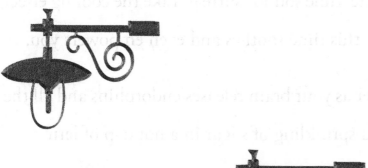

The beautiful world we live in is marred by manipulations. Anger, irreverent politeness, requests – constantly directed at us, leaving us feeling obsequious and drained.

This in turn makes us angry and we run the risk of not only damaging relationships but also ourselves.

Wreaking havoc on our self-esteem, general feeling of wellness and happiness these thoughts are simply detrimental. We would need to deploy all our physical and mental strength to bounce back.

It is then that the idea of 'me' time sounds surreal. Like the cooling effect of water on a dry arid day, this time soothes and even empowers you.

A surge of energy takes over as your brain releases endorphins and all the negativity disappears like a sprinkling of sugar in a hot cup of latte.

I am most certain that this is motivation enough and you have put this book down you will unknowingly have a smile on your lips as you realize that you have just spent some great quality 'me' time and that in the somewhat paralyzing mess you have brought some semblance of sense. ☺

Take this little 'helper' home. Make notes for each day on how much 'me time' you afforded yourself. As time goes by, consciously increase the number of 'me' minutes - you will thank yourself.

Personal Notes

Personal Notes

Personal Notes

Personal Notes

Personal Notes

Personal Notes

_____

_____

_____

_____

_____

_____

_____

_____

_____

_____

_____

Personal Notes

Personal Notes

_____

_____

_____

_____

_____

_____

_____

_____

_____

_____

Personal Notes

Personal Notes

Personal Notes

Personal Notes

Personal Notes

Personal Notes

Personal Notes

_____

_____

_____

_____

_____

_____

_____

_____

_____

_____

_____

_____

Personal Notes

Personal Notes

Personal Notes

Personal Notes

Personal Notes

Personal Notes

Personal Notes

Personal Notes

Personal Notes

Personal Notes